OF THE CONTRACT

Before you start to read this book, take this moment to think about making a donation to punctum books, an independent non-profit press,

@ https://punctumbooks.com/support/

If you're reading the e-book, you can click on the image below to go directly to our donations site. Any amount, no matter the size, is appreciated and will help us to keep our ship of fools afloat. Contributions from dedicated readers will also help us to keep our commons open and to cultivate new work that can't find a welcoming port elsewhere. Our adventure is not possible without your support.
Vive la open-access.

Fig. 1. Hieronymus Bosch, *Ship of Fools* (1490–1500)

OF THE CONTRACT. Copyright © 2017 Christopher Clifton. This work carries a Creative Commons BY-NC-SA 4.0 International license, which means that you are free to copy and redistribute the material in any medium or format, and you may also remix, transform, and build upon the material, as long as you clearly attribute the work to the authors and editors (but not in a way that suggests the authors or punctum books endorses you and your work), you do not use this work for commercial gain in any form whatsoever, and that for any remixing and transformation, you distribute your rebuild under the same license. http://creativecommons.org/licenses/by-nc-sa/4.0/

First published in 2017 by dead letter office, BABEL Working Group
an imprint of punctum books, Earth, Milky Way.
https://punctumbooks.com

The BABEL Working Group is a collective and desiring-assemblage of scholar-gypsies with no leaders or followers, no top and no bottom, and only a middle. BABEL roams and stalks the ruins of the post-historical university as a multiplicity, a pack, looking for other roaming packs with which to cohabit and build temporary shelters for intellectual vagabonds. We also take in strays.

ISBN-13: 978-1-947447-04-2 (print)
ISBN-13: 978-1-947447-05-9 (ePDF)

LCCN: 2017945437
Library of Congress Cataloging Data is available from the Library of Congress

Book design: Vincent W.J. van Gerven Oei

HIC SVNT MONSTRA

Christopher Clifton

of

the

contract

Say: "I will swear to keep the contract,
or keep silent."

Contents

*Of the Origins of the Contract · 15
Definitions · 21
Of Interpretation · 37
Consideration · 45
Of the Funding · 53
The Investment · 71
The Account · 81
The Debt · 89
Against Property · 103
Default · 107
Of the Difference · 115
Of the Void · 121
Of Finance · 127
Of the Lapse · 135
Termination · 141*

Index of Names · 147

Of the Contract

Of the Origins of the Contract

1.1.1 The contraction out of nothing that was said to be the first origination of the universe continues to express its irreducible commitments.

1.1.2 Even if conceived of as afforded by "the death of ancient stars" is such reducible to having been contracted.

1.1.3 That the contract had been founded in the origin of sunlight as perceptively discovered, whereby that which was invasively without became a source of inner meaning — with a concomitant gas to be contracted by a later age as "atmosphere to live in" — is a fundamental term that leads to vision. As provisional such term will be shown void in light of any later outcome.

1.1.4 The distance of first vision was a qualitative change that led to reason.

1.1.5 Thus the fictional first cause gave rise to reason — not what reason would contend with.

1.2.1   The origins of the contract are internal to the contract.

1.2.2   The awareness of the contract is the origin of man.

1.2.3   That "the universe is founded on the contract" is a secondary term that could be understood to signify in countless other ways than that first-given.

1.2.4   The beginning is impossible to think of but as cause for termination.

1.2.5   Even if the contract is believed to be a product of that past that it enabled such is relevant to future understanding.

1.2.6   The universe is brought to light by finance.

1.2.7   The only obligation is to name.

1.3.1 "The possession of the earth by means of naming, in exchange for an impossible transgression of the nature of the same," was an inadequate conception of the contract. It would signify however, to a consciousness of redetermination, an obligatory stage that could not signify as such to its own subject. It would come to be rephrased as "The renouncement of the world received transcends the prohibition," whereby death became a process to adhere to.

1.3.2 It was not so much the eating of the fruit that gave them knowledge of the difference, but by having been expelled from perfect ease to the uncertainty without whereby they came to understand that they could never break their law. Thus "the knowledge of good and evil" was a superficial sign of an enduring prohibition. Which did not preclude the thought that it be lifted from without: as adhered to in the work of preparation, the forbidding was named "faith" by those that followed.

1.3.3 The expulsion from that space in which all things had been received in certain safety, and obediently nurtured by the name that each was given, as it came in time to light, by prohibition; was effected by the name the same was given and adhered to, as the image of a whole that could not substitute the life that had produced it.

1.3.4 Perhaps the same was a conception that fell short because dependent on an interval of climate.

1.3.5 It was what Adam was incapable of naming that occasioned his original default, which resulted in a secondary contract to adhere to. Only later was the prospect of such breach to be conceived of as a positive event to be prepared for.

1.4.1   A term of comprehension that facilitates the world to come is only an approach that somehow signifies a future understanding. An initial understanding merely constitutes the need to pass away.

1.4.2   The expression of a fundamental term perceived the rainbow.

1.4.3   The significance of such exceeds the limited awareness it produces.

1.5.1   A term that only signifies the need for the acceptance of another term as yet to be decided may be presently observed by letting go.

1.5.2   *Allow* for the fulfilment of the contract.

1.6.1 A signature consents to keep resigning.

Definitions

2.1.1   The acceptance of a term is an awareness of the contract as renewed in the return to the beginning.

2.1.2   Liability implied by that initial understanding is a universal term-to-be-decided.

2.1.3   Thus prohibited from knowledge of the world to come, the only obligation is to name.

2.1.4   That the contract came to be cannot be reasoned.

2.1.5   *Enter the contract* to the world.

2.2.1   Everything is owing to the contract.

2.2.2   The essential operation of the contract has defined itself as funding.

2.2.3   For the most part will the contract be assumed without awareness of its fundamental role in the unfolding of the universe in which there be perception. That it cannot be a part of this unfolding to observe is what allows it to be taken thus for granted.

2.2.4   Notwithstanding the awareness of the contract is the essence of mankind.

2.2.5   The contract as discovered as the contract is the basis of the human thus contracted.

2.2.6   To speculate on that to which the contract be relation — that it be between a "god" and any "human," for example — is to make of this an object that takes place among the countlessly diverse specifications of the contract, as another mere example of contraction.

2.2.7   That to which the contract be relation disassociates from every speculation.

2.3.1 A term is a conception of the contract.

2.3.2 A term is not the cause of all that follows, but allows that cause to be.

2.3.3 A conception of the contract is enabled by the contract.

2.3.4 Its conception is not knowledge of the contract, but acceptance of the need for its ulterior fulfilment.

2.3.5 A conception of the contract is internal to the contract, and so cannot be assumed as more than merely an example of its funding operation. An example nonetheless that would be relevant to every thing contracted in the future.

2.3.6 A term is an example of the contract; or a clause that may refer to a specific obligation; or a period of time.

2.3.7 The contract is a term for that which constitutes the contract.

2.3.8 Beyond this simple act of constitution, its significance is void.

2.3.9 A term that would initiate the contract has no lasting application whatsoever.

OF THE CONTRACT

2.4.1 Every instance of the contract is the contract as a whole. The attention must be undivided always.

2.4.2 An imperative to concentrate derives from the uniqueness of each vision. There is no determination that may equally apply to all or anything that follows.

2.4.3 Independently of any other term a term will constitute the contract.

2.4.4 Every term is as the contract, of the contract, and towards another contract.

2.4.5 That a term be an expression of the contract irrespective of those past explains their intercontradiction.

2.4.6 Between the terms may be no obvious connection that would constitute the essence of the contract. This may never be consistently derived from the conjunction of the terms that have already been accepted — even if those terms could be presented in the manner of objective recognition, which they certainly cannot.

2.4.7 A term is a fulfilment of the contract, and a sign of its eventual fulfilment.

2.5.1   The contract is not fixed for once and all, but must be redefined, or reaccepted, in the wake of every instance.

2.5.2   It is not to terms already of the contract that would have to be adhered, but to ongoing termination.

2.5.3   Only by continuing acceptance of the terms may the agreement be adhered to. Definitions of a stationary contract are unable to account for what they cannot take account of. Their persistence is the basis of illusion, and illusion could prove deadly.

2.5.4   The conception of the contract as a process of contraction — not as this or that contracted — is an unfulfilled acceptance of the contract. An awareness of the contract is awareness of the need to let such go. Its conception is ongoing.

2.5.5   Adherence to the contract is the redetermination of the sense to be adhered to, in the sense that this adherence must be learnt each time anew.

2.5.6   Thus the signing of the contract is the always unintentional acceptance of the sense of an agreement to renew in terms of endless resignation.

2.5.7   The signing of the contract is the tentative acceptance of what cannot be conceived by such an instance.

2.5.8   Thus to sign is to renounce the world as given by the contract.

2.6.1   The contract was accepted in the darkness of the womb.

2.6.2   The conception of the terms, and so the entrance into life, cannot be chosen by that life itself elected.

2.6.3   *Live* according to the terms.

2.6.4   An explicit formulation of the contract is a fact of that which cannot be returned to.

2.6.5   A conscience stands in witness to the contract.

2.6.6   The inherent incompletion of the contract is an openness to other kinds of meaning.

2.6.7   The capacity to live from day to day will be dependent on an openness to other obligations. Funding may not ever be procured for once and all, but must be endlessly entreated.

2.6.8   The slow specification of the contract is the differentiation of concerns as they concern.

2.6.9   The contract must be kept in every moment. This imperative derives from the particular import of every moment, and the incomparability of any situation.

2.6.10 Survival is a process of adherence to the contract.

2.6.11 The ability to keep the terms is given by the terms.

2.6.12 *Keep* not to terms, but termination.

2.7.1　*Adhere not* to an image of the contract, nor of anything besides that presupposes the existence of the contract, but the contract of itself, as an imperative that brings the world to light in an ongoing self-fulfilment.

2.7.2　The contract is not specified by absolute conditions to adhere to, but adaptable provisions to enable.

2.7.3　To keep the contract one must learn to learn at every single turn.

2.7.4　Every term is a fulfilment of the contract.

2.8.1 An adherence to the contract is the swearing of an oath not to adhere to this or that.

2.8.2 To swear is to fulfil an obligation formed already by the contract.

2.8.3 The acceptance of the contract is in heed to its forbidding to begin with. For the matter this would signify is yet to be decided. The obedience to terms is their acceptance.

2.8.4 The decisions are not chosen, but accepted as they come. A difficult decision is of relevance to failure to perceive, and not a conflict of positions.

2.8.5 The contract is a process of contraction (to adhere to).

2.8.6 Irreversible contraction of the terms is the performance of the contract.

2.9.1   The contract would provide for any outcome.

2.9.2   The capacity to meet the unexpected is provided by the terms.

2.9.3   The worth of the provisions is impossible to measure by whatever other means than realisation.

2.9.4   No thing may appear without the contract, which is not itself a thing to be considered. That implied in the perception of whatever is could never be perceived as such directly.

2.9.5   The acceptance of the terms allows for any thing to be.

2.9.6   That to which the contract has brought access must be seen as something borrowed. A definitive account of all that is cannot be given.

2.9.7   A difficulty keeping the agreement may derive from the persistency of vision.

2.9.8   The present application of the terms will be an obstacle to future implications.

2.9.9   Functionality of terms preserves their structure, in which every one makes sense, or has a meaning; but significance is lost to such a structure.

2.9.10   The polysemous nature of the terms enables coverage.

2.9.11   The significance of such a clause will have to be decided. For the time that is its information functions.

2.10.1   The contract is perceivable by means of its contingent applications, but in no such seen directly. The conception of an absolute totality of means is an invalid application of the contract.

2.10.2   The agreement may be kept as long as active. Only by continued demonstration of specific obligations may the contract be adhered to.

2.10.3   The particulars are void — and the investment must continue.

2.10.4   The lapse of the agreement is to understand as need for further funding.

2.10.5   The universe is brought to light by signing.

2.11.1   There is no reason for the contract, in the sense that it be taken to achieve a given aim. The sole condition for whatever aim or purpose is the contract. These are consequent to such, and not its reason.

2.11.2   One is not to presuppose a space of possible occurrence, but prepare for unforeseen considerations.

2.11.3   Understanding of the contract as the source of all that is in terms of funding is not knowledge of what can or not be funded.

2.11.4   The terms provide for no specific outcome, but for "anything to come." They are provisional in such that they allow one to respond to the interminate unknown that would invalidate their temporary structure.

2.11.5   *Accept* the need to alter.

2.12.1 Awareness is both consequence and keeping of the contract.

2.12.2 The awareness becomes consciousness when taken from the drafting of the contract. As detached from the condition of the term it corresponds to the extension of an instance of default.

2.12.3 Incorporation of a fundamental term is a formation of the self.

2.12.4 The signing of the contract is no choice that may be taken or discarded. There has never been an option.

2.12.5 A term is that which frees the self from failure to perceive.

2.12.6 The acceptance of a term is an expression of consent to keep accepting the expression of the terms.

2.13.1   As considered independent of its own determinations will the contract be accepted as the promise of another kind to come. The contraction of a term, which as a deeper understanding would initiate that other kind of contract, will not satisfy the need for its ulterior fulfilment.

2.13.2   The implication of another kind of contract in the presence of some thing before unseen would be the only guarantee that such be certain.

2.13.3   The signing of the contract is what certifies the presence of all things.

2.13.4   The contractions are internal to the contract, whereby that which was without an understanding may be suddenly brought forth by an internal alteration of the contract.

2.13.5   A term is less important than the contract it determines. The necessity for such could have resulted in innumerable such terms — or at least it would appear from a perspective that seems destined to have happened.

2.13.6   That when looking back a term appears an unavoidable resultant is a given point of view that cannot lay aside its late determination.

2.13.7   Only in the predisposed contingency of hindsight may one contract seem implied within one former.

2.13.8   That that past that would appear as antecedent to the term that has enabled its appearance as a cause will also signify an undecided future.

2.14.1   A performance of the contract brings a limited potential to invest with.

2.14.2   An inefficient contract lacks a fundamental term that would decide its operation.

2.14.3   The condition for the fullest operation of the contract will be met at such time as would allow for its effective implication.

2.14.4   The condition that would guarantee the freedom to invest remains unknown to the contracted.

Of Interpretation

3.1.1 A superficial reading of the contract may induce one to conceive it as the predetermination of a world where every possible response to every possible occurrence be implied in its original conception. But between the lines that constitute this world draws an immense accountability to realise.

3.1.2 Accountability is founded in the fact that the conditions are susceptible to renegotiation.

3.1.3 The function of a term may differentiate according to the context.

3.1.4 The terms themselves are open to alternative conceptions, where an unexpected context may disclose an unintended second meaning. This however would suppose that they equate to formulations that are written to refer to, when in fact they are unique approximations that may never be repeated. The words are interchangeable, and alter what they mean as they attach themselves to singular contractions — the significance of which must be decided. (Terminology)

3.1.5 The lacunae may facilitate renewed interpretation.

3.2.1   The terms may represent a certain world to those that contemplate their subject; but to others they may signify another world to come.

3.2.2   An obstinate construction of the text extends the interest to reinforce the difference to pay.

3.2.3   Strict adherence to the terms as understood in the appearance of the world one has to live in, and the subsequent possession of the image of the same is an obstruction to the world to which they signal.

3.2.4   The significance of this or that expression of the world would be alternative expression. As human substitution for what cannot be perceived by any means that are provided, what it signifies would have to be another substitution for whatever that may mean. Such expression is subjunctive, in the sense that it would signify "if only."

3.2.5   The terms of everything must signify themselves in terms of everything.

3.3.1 There is a certain closure of the terms in the persistence of the world one has to live in. Their significance — and not their present function — is of worlds that are to come.

3.3.2 A clause defines a world in which each term performs a function. The perception that results from this in principle may endlessly extend; but its constancy depends upon an ignorance that cannot be as endlessly maintained.

3.3.3 A clause consists of statements such as "because this, then that," within a self-sustaining cycle of conclusion. Reproducing the appearance of a world that is maintained by such to live in, this interior is closed to what it cannot take account of. It may come to be disproved, or grafted into.

3.3.4 Through the maintenance of life that life is threatened.

3.3.5 The interminate refutes all propositions.

3.3.6 The abrupt interpretation of a term may draw a secondary function to facilitate survival.

3.4.1 There is a text behind each vision of "the cosmos." Interpretation redetermines the capacity to see, and so to prosper.

3.4.2 The text is not to read as a definitive instruction, but an open sensibility to meaning.

3.4.3 The covenant with Abraham had no specification to depend on, but was pertinent to all that he could ponder. The significance of stars was of the one that was impossible to realise. Notwithstanding this they symbolised a promise, that the covenant would open to such numbers.

3.4.4 As impossible to specify the covenant was taken as a covenant of faith, not strict adherence.

3.4.5 The polysemous nature of the stars is of the darkness.

3.5.1   The contract is interpreted by that which is without an understanding.

3.5.2   That which is without an understanding would interpret such a term as would produce it.

3.5.3   That which would interpret would appear as something given to return to.

3.5.4   An interpretation of the document would generate its object — like a line that would interpret.

3.5.5   Every new interpretation re-establishes the text to re-interpret.

3.5.6   A sentence would decide between two contracts.

3.6.1 Specification is a process of interior fulfilment of the contract. This fulfilment is not consequent to terms-to-be-fulfilled, but the necessity for terms-to-be-contracted. The perceptions that result from these are temporary claims to be abandoned.

3.6.2 The inherent incompletion of the contract is not such that it be qualified according or compared to a conceivable completion, which needs only to be filled; but means that any such completion has no meaning.

3.6.3 The incompletion of the contract is an opening for grace.

3.6.4 Any new interpretation is the singular contraction of a secondary term that will necessitate renewed interpretation. Such a term will be implied within the structure of the text it has made sense of. Every new interpretation opens unforeseen potential to interpret.

3.6.5 Interpretation needs interpretation.

4.3.1 The contractual resources are the flexible provisions that allow to come to terms with that which threatens to disrupt their present order.

4.3.2 Where the threat grows draws relief.

4.3.3 A fund would be available as needed.

4.3.4 The funding is attained by definition of the contract.

4.3.5 There can be no world to count on — only an unlimited liability to realise.

4.3.6 The unlimited liability invalidates all previous engagements to allow for the fulfilment of the nearest obligation.

4.3.7 A term defines a space to be decided. This can only be received as the unlimited liability that signifies the need to be attentive.

4.3.8 The space that has been opened by the signing of the contract is not given as a predetermined set of definitions or co-ordinates or properties, but infinitely opens.

4.3.9 The unlimited liability implied in the awareness of the contract is defined by every instance.

4.4.1   The unlimited liability may be realised by uncountable contingent obligations.

4.4.2   An obligation is to *let such be*.

4.4.3   Every obligation is a singular exception to the world that went before it.

4.4.4   Every good is to receive as a specific obligation, which is not to be retained as such to dwell on.

4.4.5   Obligation signifies not otherwise than this or that received consideration.

4.4.6   Every obligation is fulfilled as it arrives, in isolation.

3.7.1   An interpretation of the text cannot define what was accepted as "the contract" in the past, but its acceptance for the present.

3.7.2   The performance of the contract is not limited to this or that objective to arrive at, and may have no final aim. The "unlimited performance" is a term that will refer to its own reinterpretation.

3.7.3   The diverse interpretations are not true for every instance, but are true in every instance.

3.7.4   The contracts of the past have been implied in the awareness of the present.

Consideration

4.1.1   The contract is received as an unlimited capacity to fund or to determine.

4.1.2   Consideration is provisionally defined as without limit, but conditional to terms received as needed.

4.1.3   Consideration is "unlimited resources to depend on," but could also be conceived as an "unlimited liability to realise."

4.1.4   Funding is received in terms of unforeseen commitments.

4.1.5   The "unlimited resources" that are not to be received as ready means to be invested, but accepted in the form of obligations to adhere to, are translated as "unlimited endebtment."

4.1.6   "Unlimited liability" is defined as liability that cannot be defined without increasing.

4.2.1 The wealth that would be given by fulfilment of the terms cannot be measured in advance of such fulfilment.

4.2.2 Such a resource is impossible to number. It may only be defined by its ongoing operation. Definition of this kind can have no end — but it goes on, and must go on.

4.2.3 The contract has provisions not for that which might occur, but that which happens.

4.2.4 As the signs of future wealth, the provisions would enable the reception of what cannot be predicted.

4.2.5 The provisions are prescribed with no intention for the future, but are open to extreme interpretations.

4.2.6 "What realities may come" can be no matter of concern until they happen. The provisions only intimate an ultimate response to what they cannot take account of.

4.2.7 A provision would facilitate the unforeseen perception of the future. As a vision that precedes its own significance is blindness.

4.5.1   The existing obligations will remain conflicting visions.

4.5.2   Obligations are dissolved in termination of the contract.

4.5.3   The imperative to sign is irreducible to any one commitment; for the pressure to repay is universal.

4.5.4   Obligations are the means with which to meet the need to pay.

4.5.5   The operation of the contract draws new figures to discharge the obligations.

4.5.6   Consideration comes as an express interpretation of the contract.

4.6.1   Consideration is not something to assume, but rather something to consider.

4.6.2   Every new consideration is a promise to fulfil, and not a presence to adhere to.

4.6.3   Consideration is invested as a means to keep the contract, and let go.

4.6.4   Considerations serve as a reflection of the contract, which as nothing in itself but the prerequisite for anything must separate itself from every last consideration to continue.

4.6.5   The complete consideration is postponed as but a fictional inducement to entreat the operation of the contract.

4.7.1   That the contract is must follow that there be consideration. Irrespective of the nature of that thing, there must be something to consider.

4.7.2   That there be consideration of some kind is a condition of the contract.

4.7.3   That there be consideration is to understand to signify the contract.

4.7.4   Every figure is a promise to interpret.

Of the Funding

5.1.1 The facility is not itself a thing to be considered — as a promise for example of unlimited resources that will serve as an inducement to the signing of the contract — but is that which would allow consideration to begin with. There is nothing to distinguish what is formally referred to as "the contract" from this faculty that funds. The acceptance of its terms is how it functions.

5.1.2 Funding is received in the performance of the contract, which occurs as the expression of the terms.

5.1.3 The performance of the contract means not only its efficient operation, but fulfilment of the terms. This fulfilment would provide for any outcome.

5.1.4 The facility may not be circumscribed by every possible requirement in advance of realisation, but determines on the go, and as it has to. Thus provisionally defined by its particular examples the facility makes real.

5.1.5 The operation of the contract is the unforeseen production of the real.

5.2.1　The facility escapes the comprehension it enables. As prerequisite to things as such in general it is nothing in itself but the necessity to yield to its unthinkable conditions.

5.2.2　The presence of the contract presupposes its own funding operation. It would follow that the contract would invalidate its own determination.

5.2.3　The contract is the founding operation that has come to be accepted as the essence of the world. It is not a thing to think of, but considered nonetheless it may present itself as such. Although not adequate to that which it would seem to be the image, such an image represents a subtle shift in its ongoing operation, so that that which it would represent must signify as such in turn no longer.

5.2.4　A single definition of the contract merely signifies the same as a particular example of its (fictional) operation.

5.3.1 The facility is given as what gives consideration. It appears as such in that there be appearance, not as such or such appearance.

5.3.2 The presumption of the contract in the presence of whatever it may be must not be simplified to signify "a totality that implicates the predetermination of all possible perception," as has happened in the past. Definitions of this kind are to refer to as the obstinate remainder of a single operation of the contract, which could never be perceived as such directly. Such totality will always be conceived as but another mere example to let go of.

5.3.3 The contract is the faculty for things as such in general — not as "everything" considered, but in every thing considered.

5.3.4 The funding cannot be objective.

5.3.5 Although it be defined as an unlimited resource this form of finance is not measured in the manner of a quantitative agency to cover any need, but is the qualitative measure of all things. It is contracted out of nothing.

5.4.1 The facility provides for things not formerly provided — such as "galaxies beyond the milky way."

5.4.2 The financial operations that allow for the appearance of whatever it may be define the contract. They are only to receive in separation from what rights and obligations have continued until now.

5.4.3 The acceptance of the terms of resignation would allow for things to be.

5.4.4 To be able to receive one must *relinquish*.

5.5.1   The terms that are of relevance to funding may not specify what can or not be funded. There is nothing to preclude a future outcome. What they signify pertains to that which cannot be conceived by a contracted understanding.

5.5.2   The facility that lends is not the subject of a limit to invest with, but itself provides the limits to adhere to. There is nothing to preclude the unpredictable existence of whatever it may be — but whatever comes to be is not an option to take up, or turn away from.

5.5.3   Funding therefore cannot be reduced to a specific sum to spend on any project. It specifically defines the thing invested.

5.5.4   The sum of all that is is an impossible abstraction.

5.5.5   The facility enables not according to the means that it has ready to dispose — but by agreement.

5.5.6   There is no limit to the funding, but each fund provides a limit to adhere to.

5.5.7   A term of understanding to invest is also limit to investment.

5.5.8   Every fund is finite.

5.6.1   The funding is of singular examples, which are not to serve as funding for whatever else besides. They are contracted out of nothing, as occurrences of debt that have no substance to depend on.

5.6.2   The use of what is funded for the funding of another kind of business or concern is an abuse of the agreement.

5.6.3   Considerations such as foodstuff, clothes, apartments, and unlimited diversions are provided as required by individual contractions. Thus to live and to enjoy the world one has to come to terms without assuming what one has as had to bargain — for the price of any good is irreducible to any good besides.

5.6.4   A term would be the price of any good that would produce it out of nothing.

5.6.5   The singular enjoyment of each aspect of the world received is all that may be taken as your own.

5.7.1 Though the contract may be seen by its examples, it is not by such defined. That "a house" has been provided, in conjunction with "an automatic vehicle" to drive in, and with "food" to be consumed is not construed to mean that anything besides may be derived from their adjacent constitutions. That they are is not a consequence of conscious calculation, but of gradual acceptance of the terms.

5.7.2 A fund is not reducible to something-to-consider. As contracted out of nothing, it is that which has allowed some thing to be; which is not to be reduced to parts or precedents. The image of "an atom" is a mere approximation to begin with, and so cannot be the ground of the emergence of whatever else may be.

5.7.3 A stone is an expression of the universe to equal any star. There is no precedence, nor order to adhere to.

5.7.4 The facility provides in spite of everything provided.

5.8.1   The facility implies determination; where the fund that it concedes for either this or that proposal presupposes the contraction of a term by which the sense of such is settled. The term itself is funding. The "unlimited resources" are not open to the will and inclination of the subject (which must constantly expose itself to redetermination). The consequence of which is the negation of quotidian concerns: though the subject lose control, the need to exercise control is also lifted. While attentive to the terms there is no worry.

5.8.2   The objects of investment are not precedent to funding, but suppose it.

5.8.3   Funding is not granted in accordance to the will of one already predetermined, but by terms of the agreement. Thus the difficulty met with by deliberate requests for further funding.

5.8.4   To persist in an objective would be reason for a freeze on further funding.

5.8.5   The funding may be frozen by a cause by which a consciousness be held to all remaining obligations. Situations of this kind are to be recognised in anguish.

5.8.6   A contractual dysfunction leads to interest.

5.9.1 Funding may be endlessly received, as long as focus is maintained in its disinterested investment, and not drawn towards protecting what has come to be in consequence of previous investment.

5.9.2 Only passively may funding be accepted by the one who would invest it. It cannot be decided in accordance with a will that would invest it as it pleases, but decided stage by stage as obligation.

5.9.3 The funding is conceded by allowing it to draw against all interests. It is not to be assumed therefore as granted, but to ask in every instance.

5.9.4 The facility would function as absolved from the contention that results from the persistence of possession.

5.9.5 The terms are contradictory to all that may belong to any person. The facility provides to those that give themselves away.

5.10.1　There is "I" because there is a contract. I cannot decide on my acceptance of the contract, and the fact that I am able to imagine that I could presumes the contract has already been accepted. In the absence of this fact there would be nothing to account for.

5.10.2　The funding is contracted for whatever it may be in terms of conscience.

5.10.3　The implication of my conscience differentiates my presence from the presence of whatever else the contract has provided, such as: such or such a bird, or such a cloud, or such a ray, or such a flower.

5.10.4　That the funding be received is not a matter of free choice.

5.11.1   The contract is to operate in terms of resignation.

5.11.2   To negotiate the terms is not to argue either way, but to accept them as directed.

5.11.3   The facility may never be controlled by any means that it has formally provided. It is not to be controlled, but given into.

5.11.4   The performance of the contract is received as an ongoing expectation. The facility facilitates such yielding such diverse consideration — which appears as an incentive to continue.

5.11.5   The entreatment must continue, irrespective of whatever has already been provided by the contract.

5.11.6   Not for this or that, the entreatment is disinterested concern for what exceeds the understanding.

5.11.7   *Give up everything* for nothing.

5.12.1 The need for funding is the need for understanding.

5.12.2 The production of the universe by funding, which derives from an originary lapse in terms that indicate their ultimate fulfilment, whereby that which is agreed as insufficient to account for what it stands for is a promise to repay the same in future generations, will proceed by way of endless resignation.

5.12.3 The funding cannot constitute a permanent foundation to depend on. The reality produced by its ungraspable contraction must be taken as a debt to be absolved from. All reality gives way to the necessity to pay.

5.12.4 There could be nothing if not given by the contract. But the insufficient funding means that nothing in particular is guaranteed to be. The guarantee refers to that, regardless what it be, there must be something to consider. Thus the funding is assured, but not that funded.

5.12.5 That there be something to consider is condition of the contract.

5.13.1	The term that starts the funding operation is irrelevant to each of the specifically invested operations that result from its spontaneous contraction. There can be no valid reference to terms that have contracted in the past, but an ongoing termination; which may nonetheless stand still. Lack of funding will eventuate from conscious interruption in the process to adhere to.

5.13.2	The facility withdraws from every formal definition. Thus the terms that would appear to comprehend its operation are already left behind by its ongoing operation. Such is contrary to things, which it has nonetheless determined.

5.13.3	The funding is contingently decided.

5.13.4	The nature of the funding is provided by the terms, but not the nature of that funded. This depends upon empirical observation, which is not to be relied on.

5.13.5	The funding is a fundamental process that must always be supposed in the existence of whatever field of reference; not a thing to be referred to, but supposed by any thing that is referred to.

5.13.6	Every fund that is contracted is implied in the ongoing formulation of the contract.

5.14.1 That from which the funding has arrived would be impossible to know by any funded apprehension.

5.14.2 The facility as such is irreducible to figures of that past that presuppose its own existence. The validity of precedent refers to the importance of reflection.

5.14.3 That the funding is in general, and in each of its examples, somehow signifies a universe distinct from than that in which had been enabled its emergence.

5.14.4 While not figures of a gross accumulation, the expression of the terms implies the funding that has happened in the past. The capacity to fund is exponential.

5.14.5 That the funding has no origin in anything that came about by funding, nor in anything at all is for the endlessly embedded understanding an imperative to yield. It may signify to such an understanding as provided by the same that it may never be intended.

5.14.6 The facility received exceeds that funded.

5.15.1 The implications of the funding for whatever may be funded in the future are impossible to know before such happens. What however can be "known," in the reflection of the present situation, is that that which has been funded presupposes the financial operations that had brought the world to light in former ages.

5.15.2 That a figure be recorded on a page of the account book is significant perhaps for the contraction of another kind of funding.

5.15.3 What a fund that is accepted may facilitate in future is for future generations to take hold of.

5.15.4 The facility is always uncommitted.

5.16.1   The facility forbids; and the forbidding guarantees the matter funded.

5.16.2   That which the forbidding guarantees is this or that, but not another situation.

5.16.3   The forbidding guarantees a situation, in that what appears appears to be consistent. Any breach of the forbidding would dissolve the situation under question — the result of which is not to be predicted.

5.16.4   The guarantee of the validity of something is considered the forbidding of what cannot be conceived of for the moment.

5.16.5   The forbidding is conceived of as a promise to repay.

5.17.1 The significance of terms is their forbidding to begin with. While they promise future funding, they necessitate restraint from such at present.

5.17.2 The forbidding is a fundamental blindness — which has nonetheless enabled one to see.

5.17.3 The forbidding is adhered to in the work of preparation.

The Investment

6.1.1 The return on an investment is no matter of concern for the investor.

6.1.2 Investment is determined by the fund that is invested. With no freedom to invest in whatsoever it would please must the investor be prepared to leave whatever they have known before behind them. For the funds are not decided in accordance to the world that is, but world that would become.

6.1.3 Funding may be granted to invest for an alternative to live in. What that world to come might look like is no possible concern for the investor, who looks only to enable.

6.1.4 That which is left out of the account is an immeasurable return on the investment.

6.1.5 The investments of the contract are for anyone to come.

6.2.1   The terms of the investment are not objects of investment, and impossible to clarify in terms of any actual investment.

6.2.2   The source of funding cannot be accepted as an object of investment of the same.

6.2.3   Terms may never be invested into terms, but into matters of concern.

6.2.4   The facility allows for only actual investments, not intangible designs of an uncertain speculation. There is nothing to contain the source of funding in the future, but the fund for now is finite.

6.2.5   The acceptance of a term precedes reception of the means thereby invested.

6.2.6   Only one thing at one time may be invested.

6.3.1 That the presently invested be objectively retained for use in future situations would invalidate the faculty that funded the investment to begin with. This will nonetheless retain the term that granted such when functional in future.

6.3.2 The potential to invest is instantaneous, and cannot be transferred, or left for later.

6.3.3 All credit is of limited duration.

6.3.4 A reality that comes about by credit will depend upon that credit to continue.

6.3.5 Credit may recede without another situation to replace the one left owing; in which case that situation will be difficult to bear.

6.3.6 An investment will remain as something owing in itself, and thereby signify the need for a renewal of the contract.

6.3.7 Credit is of precedence to swearing.

6.4.1 The investment of the funding will take form as sworn adherence to the term by which that funding has been granted.

6.4.2 An investment is an oath.

6.4.3 An oath is that which holds to the agreement. One may not therefore be held to such in future — though this oath may be construed in other ways than first intended.

6.4.4 Such an oath is not a statement to adhere to, but the manner of adherence to the contract.

6.4.5 A specific affirmation is a promise to adhere made in adherence to the contract.

6.5.1 Only as an unresolved provision will an oath concern the future. As an oath it is of pertinence to that which it adheres to in the present. It is not to be referred to as a promise of intention, but may come to be accounted for according to a circumstance of which it has no notion. The sense of any oath is always open.

6.5.2 Left behind as proof of an adherence to the contract, and as freely given means by which another may gain entry to the contract, the expression of an oath is a specific affirmation for the future.

6.5.3 That which has been signified may only be conceived of by resigning, which would signify in turn the need for signing. A sign is the expression of a promise to repay, which at the same time serves as payment.

6.5.4 A sign is an injunction to invest for the uncertainty it points to.

6.5.5 Swearing to adhere to a condition of the contract the investor leaves to other understandings.

6.6.1   The potential to invest is not compatible with any inclination to possess the thing invested, nor with any selfish aim, nor last objective. Terms are given to facilitate what cannot be conceived by the investor.

6.6.2   That the funding be available depends on the relinquishment of previous investments.

6.6.3   Investments are let go, and left for future generations to make use of.

6.6.4   The return on an investment is for consciences to come.

6.7.1 As the funding is impossible to save for reinvestment, the account will be a record of all actual investments. These however may eventuate as subject to investment in the future.

6.7.2 A provisional account may thus be given as a source of future funding.

6.7.3 To invest is to provision with a name to be recorded on a page of the account, for the contraction of return in terms of future understanding.

6.7.4 What the figures of the past may come to signify in terms of reinvestment is impossible to speculate at present. However, that these figures be susceptible to reconsideration may be taken from the quality of worth in their formation.

6.7.5 The sense of prohibition is condition for the freedom to invest within the present.

6.8.1   The worth of an investment is the only guarantee that it be valid to begin with — as the promise of return on that investment.

6.8.2   The worth is incommensurable with something to consider.

6.8.3   The quality of worth that may in no way be accounted is the only guarantee for the protection of that given to make use of.

6.8.4   The quality of worth may be conceived of as a promise to fulfil in future ages; thus significant of worlds that are to come.

6.8.5   Not as something signified, the quality of worth is the significance itself of something given. This significance is open.

6.9.1   The quality of worth may only last for the duration of the term by which a thing has been provided. In the subsequent fixation of this quality this quality escapes the thing contracted. Funding cannot be set down to be translated, or transferred, by any reason.

6.9.2   As detached from the financial operation that produced the thing in question will it be of worth no longer. A worthless thing however may yet constitute the focus of some future operation.

6.9.3   A worthless debt may yet attract more funding.

6.9.4   That which is to pay, as well as that which would enable one to pay the same is signified by worth.

6.9.5   An awareness of the worth is an awareness of the contract.

6.10.1 An investment may facilitate another understanding to invest with.

6.10.2 All that is required is an awareness of the indetermination of the terms of the investment, and an openness to reinterpretation.

6.10.3 The source of wealth is endless.

The Account

7.1.1   The nature of the debt may be accounted for in terms of a reflection on the method of accounting.

7.1.2   At every stage of the ongoing evolution of accounting has the nature of that taken to account been universally transfigured; in the wake of which has followed a numerical expansion of that nature.

7.1.3   The formulation of the contract and accountancy were not to differentiate when writing was invented. This inseparable event was only later to give rise to different manners of narration, such as "literature," and "finance," and "the law," as well as "science." Their contraction at the end of this historical occurrence may again give rise to other kinds of story.

7.1.4   The facts in the account book are in fact interpretations of the contract.

7.1.5   Only in its strange and disconnected taking place a fact is valid.

7.2.1 According to the functional requirements of the contract is a qualitative method of accountancy to follow. As instructed by the terms that are of relevance to debt this is a process of intense negotiation.

7.2.2 The accountant is in other words to utilise a single-entry method of accounting that arrives at separate figures of that owed without equating any one to any other, and records them as received in such a way as to allow for an extreme interpretation, by whatever world to come (without accounting for that future). Such a method corresponds to strict adherence to the contract. It can have as such no end.

7.2.3 The contraction of a debt will be recorded on a page of the account book — to defer towards the audit of a future understanding. The account is thus the form of the ongoing formulation of the contract. The delayed interpretation of such figures of account may be conceived as the fulfilment of the terms thereby invested.

7.2.4 The accountant is to separately take note of every term that is concluded.

7.2.5 The secondary terms are to be written as received.

7.2.6 That "an entry may in future be interpreted to signify what cannot be accounted for for now" will be a fundamental premise of this method of accounting.

7.3.1   This qualitative method comes to terms with externalities that could not be accounted for by previous commitments.

7.3.2   That a figure of account can only signify what cannot be accounted for for now means that the sense of the account cannot be settled.

7.3.3   It is not that the account is incomplete, but insufficient to account for what it cannot take account of it may signify diversely from the way it was conceived when first recorded. Later entries may requalify the sense of all preceding estimations.

7.3.4   Every entry is a record of receipt of what is only to behold as but a promise to interpret. The capacity to fund is not explicitly contained in the account book, but is signified by statements left increasingly unclear.

7.3.5   That which such an entry comes to signify will have to be repaid by the contraction of a deeper understanding. That a debt has been accounted for by any final figure means that such has been received, and not how such may be remitted.

7.3.6   How to pay is a concern that is impossible to answer in advance of an eventual repayment. There is nothing to suggest a way to terminate the presence of a debt in which a consciousness be endlessly abandoned.

7.3.7   "Quantitative debt" would be a quality that indicates the pressure to repay.

7.4.1   Recognition of a debt may not for now be recognition of the worth that it may nonetheless be sign of.

7.4.2   An entry is a sign of that which has to be accounted for in future — whether recognised as such, or misinterpreted to mean that such has taken an account of such already.

7.4.3   That which cannot be accounted cannot even be perceived as not accounted.

7.4.4   That which is external to the field of calculation of the debt may have no reference beyond such substitution. To account for it would need the constitution of another kind of contract.

7.4.5   That which is excluded from the lines of the account may come to light by means of signing.

7.4.6   That which is accounted is internal to the world and therefore given to make use of; but as recognised as debt to be completely handed over.

7.4.7   The fiction of an immanent account is the result of one mistaken estimation.

7.5.1 One could imagine that a term that is conserved in written form upon a single piece of paper be the substitute for various new things and situations; where a primary exchange of a particular occasion be repeated by another set of hands for something other than intended, which proceeds to the exchange of countless other situations, in an open-ended space of correspondence. However, as removed from the reality that underlies its reason, which had even as conceived been insufficient to account for what it stood for, this equivalence appears as a complete equivocation, which will only be maintained as long as trusted. Such a space would thus collapse as soon as doubted.

7.5.2 The significance or worth of any promissory note will be reduced by the effects of countersigning.

7.5.3 The value of exchange is an expression of the same that could in principle extend forever outwards. As a mere approximation to begin with, this autonomous expansion is a reckless imposition that must fail to take account of what it cannot take account of; which it follows would invalidate its endless calculation.

7.5.4 The unlimited liability will make of the within a figure owing. The demand will not postpone itself forever. One will have to come to terms — to pay the difference.

7.5.5 To multiply a fund to try to overcome a reoccurring crisis is to reinforce the difference that constitutes its cause.

7.5.6 To calculate the funding as a thing is to conceal the very question.

7.5.7 The interminate cannot be bought with money.

7.6.1 The possibility that something be exchangeable for something is reducible to absence of attention.

7.6.2 In the space of the account there is no precedence of any one example to another, and no figure may reduce to any other.

7.6.3 The fact that every cause is an effect directly opens to the principle of insufficient reason.

7.6.4 The narration must assume no set relation between any given fact and any other, but record the incommensurable appearances of debt as they are given to make use of.

7.6.5 The opening causation goes from this because of that to this caused only.

7.6.6 The figures must be kept apart in order to allow for future entries.

7.6.7 That a figure be reduced to its constituents will constitute an error of accounting.

7.7.1   The need to reach a figure is ongoing, irrespective of what figures have been drawn to such an end.

7.7.2   A figure must be reached. Not the figure of a total, which would satisfy the need to render payment once for all — for such need is universal, and impossible to figure absolutely, in that nothing of the kind could cover all that has or has not been provided. Every figure has been borrowed; which must mean that there will always be a greater need to pay.

7.7.3   It is impossible to calculate a figure of the kind that would release the self from every obligation.

7.7.4   To settle the account would need an infinite repayment.

7.8.1 Accounting comes to terms with what remains as a result of such a process. The return on an investment is no matter of concern for the investor.

7.8.2 Any figure that is reached is to refer to as the coming to account of that which troubled the relation, by which that which it relates concerns no longer.

7.8.3 The figures are the fatal comprehensions of once immanent concerns, set down as clauses.

7.8.4 A promissory note will stay susceptible to strange interpretations.

The Debt

8.1.1 Having from the contract, and unable to accede to things directly in themselves, there may be nothing else than debt to take account of.

8.1.2 Other than the evidence of debt there may be nothing to refer to.

8.1.3 The quality of debt transcends all previous distinctions, such as "good" and "bad," "poor" and "wealthy," "real" and "illusive." But this quality itself as such has nothing to contrast with.

8.1.4 Consciousness is consciousness of debt.

8.1.5 That there be nothing else than debt for any subject to account for is a matter of concern that every subject is required to come to terms with.

8.1.6 To recognise the debt will be to recognise the need for recognition as ongoing.

8.2.1　Every thing is borrowed, in the sense of guaranteed by an unspecified necessity to pay.

8.2.2　A dependency to debt that may appear to be substantial may continue for a time of peace of mind until its seemingly unlimited extension be revealed as based on nothing.

8.2.3　Otherwise with nothing to depend on, the contraction of a debt provides a temporary ground on which a consciousness may settle. Such is groundless in itself, and will require an operation of refinance. The necessity to pay is of the void that would invalidate contemporary reason. It is not to be explained as such away, but given into.

8.2.4　That which is to pay is not a figure of that owed — but is the void that would invalidate all figures of repayment.

8.2.5　The pressure to repay is an unreasonable demand to give up everything for nothing.

8.2.6　All as debt needs funding.

8.2.7　There is nothing to depend on whatsoever.

8.3.1   The financial operations that facilitate the presence of the world thus also signify that such is of the nature of endebtment.

8.3.2   Nothing is external to the field of the account of debt contracted. To have taken an account of the beginning of the world would be to make of it another mere example of endebtment.

8.3.3   The capacity for finance is conceived as an original endebtment.

8.3.4   Not only debt perceived, but the perception of that debt is debt itself to be acknowledged as outstanding.

8.3.5   Not only what you hear, but that you hear has been provided by the contract. The facility facilitates its own facilitation.

8.4.1   Debt received is anything. Not anything in such that this or that would make no difference, in that anything at all would equal anything at all in a perception of indifference; but anything in such that, like no other, it could never have been written to refer to in advance of its particular contraction. The varieties of debt cannot be listed to begin with.

8.4.2   Understanding of the debt as such in general may have no determination on particular endebtments, like "that apple on that plate." For that apple on that plate has been decided by a single operation of the contract.

8.4.3   Something may exist for the duration of the term by which that thing has been decided.

8.4.4   The quality of debt in something given may suggest that it has no secure foundation, so that even its existence may be doubted. Only that there be a debt is all that may be certain — that is, any debt at all.

8.4.5   That there be the presence of some debt is a condition of the contract.

8.4.6   The evidence of debt must be accepted as it is, and not explained as such away.

8.5.1 The debt appears to manifest itself as without cause.

8.5.2 There can be no recollection of the terms — only present lack of funding. This predicament is not to be disputed, but accepted as the fact that one exists, which fact has never been a matter of free choice. The mandatory terms of this existence are so stringently implied that they are everywhere at once, and yet irreparably behind one. Their restriction may however be relieved by the contraction of another obligation. Though the debt be absolute, it may be financed.

8.5.3 That the terms escape the consciousness provided by the same may lead that consciousness to calculate the presence of the debt as if that debt were independent of the contract.

8.5.4 Although one may arrive at terms to terminate the petty obligations that arise from time to time, it is impossible to terminate the presence of the debt as such completely. The necessity for finance to absolve from obligations that have come to be perceived is not reducible to figures of the kind that are progressively demanded.

8.5.5 Payment may be reached by resignation.

8.6.1 The origin of debt cannot be fathomed.

8.6.2 Understanding of the origin of debt would be another mere example to absolve from.

8.6.3 That to which the subject be endebted is impossible to state without it turning into debt itself contracted. Thus the debt is not to "god," nor to "the market," nor to "cosmic evolution," nor whatever.

8.6.4 It may however be supposed that debt is owing to "the contract."

8.6.5 To understand the contract as the origin of debt is to reduce the same to debt thereby contracted.

8.6.6 That to which the universe is owed is only recognised as yet to be accepted.

8.7.1   An inadequate repayment may be understood to signify inadequate acceptance.

8.7.2   To pay is to accept another term that would allow some thing to be.

8.7.3   That which is outstanding — such as acid in the oceans, or the melting of the icecaps — may be suddenly discharged by the contraction of a fund to be invested.

8.7.4   The appearance of the world to which and in which the endebted is obliged may be abruptly shown invalid by another more believable appearance.

8.7.5   Payment is in any case a promise of repayment.

8.7.6   The need to reach agreement is ongoing.

8.7.7   The pressure to repay drives termination.

8.7.8   It matters not how much one has to pay, but that one pays; and that the payments be ongoing.

8.7.9   Anything may serve as a repayment. To assume the same as something that belongs to any subject is to fall into an instance of default.

8.7.10 There is no end to final payment.

8.8.1   The debt cannot be paid by its own substance.

8.8.2   That the debt reduce to debt would be an error of accounting.

8.8.3   The debt is irreducible in terms of what it may or may not stand for.

8.8.4   That an instance of the debt be owed to debt breaks down all meaning.

8.8.5   To reduce the debt to debt is an invalid operation of the contract. Any instance of the debt may be more valid than another notwithstanding.

8.8.6   That an instance of the debt be irreducible to debt cannot preclude that it be set aside by any other instance of endebtment.

8.8.7   A debt is irreducible, but may become dissolved in the contraction of another obligation.

8.8.8   "Debt reduction" is production of more debt.

8.9.1   There is no manner to return the debt left owing.

8.9.2   As the irreversible contraction of the past a debt may never be returned to where it came from.

8.9.3   The debt is not and cannot be attributed to any other thing nor other person; but recorded as received it is accounted for by future understanding.

8.9.4   To determine that received as equal such or such, or owing to whoever, or whatever, so that that which is received could be returned to where it came from, may be recognised as mere equivocation. That the debt could be reduced at all is relative to finance.

8.9.5   The debt is irreversible. It cannot be returned — but may be financed.

8.9.6   The question of from what the debt derives is that of relevance to payment.

8.10.1 That the debt is a production of the contract is accounted for in terms of a production of the same.

8.10.2 The origin of debt is always precedent to conscience. It may never be supposed that it could ever be the object of such conscience. But the fact of this may constitute an object of this kind, and be of relevance to debt received in future.

8.10.3 That the origin of debt cannot be known may have no bearing on the fact that it be knowingly accepted.

8.10.4 The only manner to refer to that from out of which a debt has been received is an expression of the void that voids all reference.

8.10.5 Debt is indication of the void from which it came, which would invalidate its present distribution.

8.10.6 An acknowledgement of debt is an acknowledgement of terms to be accepted.

8.10.7 Debts are cleared by finance, but the finance comes to pass in terms of other obligations to adhere to.

8.10.8 That the terms of the relation have already always past leaves the relation undecided. There is nothing to return to but to ask for the conditions of the contract.

8.11.1 "Debt" refers to "everything."

8.11.2 That everything is owed implies a subject.

8.11.3 Given as a comprehensive picture of the world the debt itself contains the mode in which the subject is to act to meet the interest. Any debt implies the debtor.

8.11.4 The structure of the debt is a division of the self into an endless field of separate obligations; which as points to be referred to, which reciprocally consolidate the ultimate identity encumbered by the same, may be discharged by termination of the contract. A restructuring of debt would presuppose another subject.

8.11.5 Subject is an insufficient term.

8.11.6 The obliged to keep the contract is created by the same.

8.11.7 The identity contracted is a single iteration of an endless alteration.

8.11.8 The financial operations draw the self outside the self, in recreation of the subject.

8.11.9 The endless separation of the inside from without moves the within towards an ever farther outside.

8.11.10 Debt cannot be paid, except by coming to new terms, in a fulfilling recommitment, which in any case falls short.

8.12.1   The financial operations that absolve the self from worldly obligations are themselves not of the order of this world. So to speak, they are to pray for.

8.12.2   From an irredeemable prehistory the present debt remains without a limit to refer to as the principle to pay. The diversions of investment would appear to have no end for the endebted understanding. And the only means to pay would be the ultimate release from obligations that is thought about in fictional accounts of "what comes after"; which as death to that which thinks mean less than nothing.

8.12.3   A figure would be reached in termination of the subject.

8.12.4   Debt may be reducible in terms of separation from what cannot be returned to.

8.12.5   The relevance of death to debt is taken to refer to an impossible return of that left owing.

8.13.1 That to which one has not come to terms is also that to which remains to be contracted — or to pay.

8.13.2 Debt is to receive as a unique consideration, and a promise to repay.

8.13.3 Having from that signifies what cannot be perceived as such directly, every instance of the debt implies a promise of unthinkable importance.

8.13.4 Every payment is a promise to repay.

8.13.5 As a sign of an eventual repayment, every debt is to be written to reread in terms of unforeseen fulfilment.

8.13.6 A debt may be referred to as a promise that would signify a consciousness to come.

Against Property

9.1.1 "Property" is founded on an ancient acceptation of a term become fixated. The expression of the same in terms of legal recognition of that owned is a perpetual construction that dissimulates the sense of what it stands for.

9.1.2 The postulate of property assumes that something tangible may constitute an origin that validates itself as independent of the universe in which it has arisen.

9.1.3 Property may constitute an obvious foundation, whereby funding for whatever else be given in relation to that principal invested. An intentional extension of the measure of the same however constitutes a failure to adhere to the conditions of the contract.

9.1.4 Default may be defined as the possession of the universe contracted.

9.2.1 Rather than a pure appropriation, the contraction of a term is an occurrence of endebtment.

9.2.2 Contraction is assumption of a debt to be discharged, and not secure appropriation of what threatened to disrupt the field of consciousness within which an existence was protected.

9.2.3 The pressure to repay is not an object of potential domination, but an unfulfilled relation to resign to.

9.2.4 Property invalidates the contract.

9.2.5 Any ownership of debt is an internal contradiction.

9.2.6 Funding cannot operate in face of the possession of that given to make use of.

9.3.1 The identity contracted to adhere to that which funds is but an instance of adherence, which is not to be adhered to howsoever.

9.3.2 The identity is given by the contract. When whatever be reduced to "my legitimate possession" my identity disrupts the operation of the contract. Who I am invalidates whoever I may be.

9.3.3 Everything I own is therefore everything I owe.

9.3.4 Reality perceived as that belonging to an incidental subject must be recognised as groundless. Only finance may resolve a situation of untenable default (as here depicted).

9.4.1   Property equates to the perception of whatever it may be.

9.4.2   There will always be a tendency to own whatever thing has been provided.

Default

10.1.1 Debt is to be understood as always overdue. Meaning that it comes too late — and always as an instance of default.

10.1.2 Every human tends by definition to default. This cannot be avoided absolutely. But by passively accepting the uncommon terms of judgement, as they come to be expressed, in resignation, the infliction of the punishment is ceaselessly remitted.

10.1.3 The avoidance of default is to be ceaselessly procured by the acceptance of new terms that stand in payment. A reduction of the difference that threatens to deprive the self of everything is merely a reprieve in an ongoing termination.

10.1.4 An apparent absolution would in any case be shown to be an actual default.

10.1.5 Every full and final payment must be recognised as merely a delay in an unceasable proceedings. It is only in this way that the default may be avoided.

10.1.6 There can be no end to payment.

10.2.1   The persistence of default is an unwillingness to question.

10.2.2   Unavoidable default, in that it come and come again despite all efforts to adhere to the conditions of the contract, and regardless of whichever debt is held to be in question, is perhaps the only way to understand the rather difficult idea of that the void cannot be voided.

10.2.3   The avoidance of default is a continuous concern for the endebted understanding. The intentional rejection of that claimed is preparation for the purely unintentional acceptance of the secondary terms of absolution. Understanding of the need for validation would be requisite for any kind of valid understanding.

10.2.4   Validation is a process of internal understanding of the contract.

10.2.5   A concept is an instance of contractual awareness; but as taken from its instance and externally applied as a generic understanding it will constitute an instance of invalid occupation.

10.2.6   The persistence of a fund is an invalid proposition. The occurrence of default is a derivative of insufficient terms.

10.3.1 The conditions of first access to whatever it may be may be ignored in the enjoyment of that given. To adhere to the conditions would require the pain of parting from whatever has provided one with comfort.

10.3.2 Default may be defined as the neglect of the conditions. This neglect will coincide with the suspension of resources.

10.3.3 Difficulty comes when the facility that funds no longer functions. For example, when the funding funds the funding operation will result its own unthinkable dysfunction.

10.3.4 That the finance finance finance makes no sense.

10.3.5 The refusal of financial intervention on the grounds of past investment, in that subsequent possession of the same must disallow its operation to continue, may be seen in such a manner as to indicate its imminent resumption.

10.3.6 Disregard for the conditions, in that such or such an object be assumed as independent of the contract, leads to permanent default and unrelenting prosecution. The conditions are that nothing be received in kind with interest, and that nothing be without them.

10.4.1 Default is a condition that takes root in the forgetting of the contract. Its forgetting means not only its persistence out of mind, but its inadequate conception to begin with.

10.4.2 The terms that are forgotten are inadequate conceptions that continue to enable the presumption of a world without awareness.

10.4.3 The contract is forgotten in such instances of questionless intent that take the world that is for granted.

10.4.4 Lack of recognition of the debt thereby mistaken for a permanent foundation to depend on is the clearest indication that the contract be forgotten.

10.4.5 The forgetting of the contract corresponds to the forgetting of the difference-to-pay, whereby it seems as if the world did not depend on the conditions of the contract. This is not to be received as if the contract were itself the so-called difference.

10.4.6 Forgotten terms are such that have produced an expectation that consistently falls short of what they stand for. Any recognition of the difference will constitute an instance of repayment.

10.4.7 Forgotten terms are grounds for prosecution. To avoid the countless consequences leading from default it is imperative to ask for further finance. Loss of expectation would eventuate from any operation of that finance.

10.4.8 The fact of falling short may lead to endless prosecution, where the judgement is eternally postponed.

10.4.9 Attendance is required for sentence hearing.

10.5.1 Possession is default; perception error.

10.5.2 Whether the received consideration be acknowledged in itself, or as a promise of fulfilment, is decisive in the question of the presence of default.

10.5.3 Either keep the thing considered, or the contract; in the sense of either letting the fulfilment of the terms, or holding on to the appearance of the world (as prosecution).

10.5.4 Rather than a source of obligation, which is yet and ever yet to be determined, the beginning of the world may be received as something settled for a subject in default; which in consequence continues to assume the same and asks no valid question. But according and attentive to the fundamental void the faithful draws the deadline forward.

10.5.5 Pride protects its place within the image of the world — not defending this itself, but by upholding the whole image.

10.5.6 The variations of the presence of default are without number. It will be difficult to see as such in every situation.

10.5.7 An excuse may not be pleaded. Every instance of default implies an absence of awareness.

10.6.1 It is impossible to set aside an inefficient contract. Though a contract be invalid, there is nothing else to stand on.

10.6.2 A term that would decide upon the nature of default is always lacking.

10.6.3 The guarantee is in the sense that the insolvent will submit to "force not specified" (until they be forgiven).

10.7.1 *Draw to basic terms,* when feeling anxious. (For example, when the pressure comes to pay, you are not able.) *Concentrate on breathing.* Another term will come.

Of the Difference

11.1.1 The terms are insufficient to account for what they stand for. There will always be a difference to pay.

11.1.2 The difference may never be reduced as such, but only given into.

11.1.3 An estimation of the difference is not to be arrived at by the means of calculation; but by payment. Yet repayment comes up short in any instance.

11.1.4 The difference-to-pay is to be understood in terms of separation from the world that was provided.

11.1.5 The contract is renewed in recognition of the difference.

11.2.1 The interminate is that to which one has not come to terms; and that which threatens that which is.

11.2.2 The interminate without can have no meaning.

11.2.3 One will have to come to terms with an unreasonable demand.

11.2.4 The difference will threaten to disrupt the way of life of the endebted understanding, to eventually enforce another payment; in default of which the conscience is increasingly uneasy.

11.2.5 The debtor is in every case in question.

11.2.6 The demand comes from without an understanding.

11.2.7 The unreasonable demand creates a figure out of nothing.

11.2.8 Payment happens.

11.3.1   That the finance is to operate in terms of understanding that approximate, but cannot comprehend the so-called difference, which endlessly defers itself by nature, and in consequence determine the remainder of a debt that is inseparable from all that is in such or such an era; is itself to be considered as a temporary ground on which to settle. The financial operations are as relevant to terms of its continued operation inconsistent, but effective. The facility will have to be entreated always otherwise, and always to begin with. There is nothing to depend on.

11.3.2   The facility works only as enabled by the difference. With no room by which to move it would not function. Adequation would be infinite, and nothing would be realised.

11.3.3   Inadequation of the terms leads to ongoing operation of the contract.

11.3.4   Like an exponential promise of production, could the difference be said to be the cause of future funding. The support received is always only finite.

11.3.5   The aporia returns; for even the most proximate without would be disclosed as a result of the discordance of the contract, the sense of which will signify a fundamental term that is to come to meet the difference; which though pressured by the difference would consist of an interior fulfilment. Though prefigured, such a term would be completely unforeseen.

11.3.6   The image left will have to be forsaken. For even in the instant of contraction it was only an approach to that which cannot be imagined.

11.4.1 The interminate necessitates an open sensibility to meaning that may passively discern all things as separate and singular, and as they are themselves in their appearance; not a preconceived idea of a totality that arrogates itself in an illusion of preponderance, where everything would seem to be submissive to the will that has contracted to fulfil it. Or at least until it wakes from such delusion.

11.4.2 The interminate is not to be commanded, nor to even be perceived by an identity that otherwise imagines. It will always overcome. Although not known it may appear to be the source of the forbidding of the image of the same.

11.4.3 The forbidding is impossible to heed, in that an image it condemns is unavoidably implied in its contingent formulation.

11.4.4 The terms are always given to adhere to. Their obedience precedes their comprehension.

11.5.1 The difference invalidates the options set before one. One may only come to terms with the interminate demand. Of default there is no obvious solution.

11.5.2 The interminable approach to the interminate without is an interminable release from obligations.

11.5.3 The interminate necessitates the void, whereby the void is an expression of the difference.

11.5.4 The difference may never be reduced by any figure of repayment. There is always more to pay.

Of the Void

12.1.1 That which it would signify invalidates a figure of repayment.

12.1.2 The terms of payment are to ceaselessly renew in terms of reinterpretation.

12.2.1 Attention to the source of the validity of any situation, which is not to be conceived of as "eternal," is less drawn to an objective as withdrawn from all objectives. A decision to grant finance in the world that it would suddenly dissolve is contradiction. Only death may lift the burden.

12.2.2 Termination is the essence of the void.

12.3.1   That which is perceptible at present is a fragile indication of the nature of the void.

12.3.2   Only in the instant of its unforeseen contraction is an observation valid.

12.3.3   The validity of such an operation as that opens the perception to a consequence that could not be by any means foreseen, may not extend to that perception. It may nonetheless remain as most conducive to whatever it may signify to other understandings.

12.3.4   The validity of such or such an image of the world will coincide with the irreparable effect of termination; whereby that which is perceived as such is recognised as fatefully discharged, and so no longer a concern.

12.3.5   A sentence will be valid for as long as it be open to the process of revision. For as soon as it has settled into any kind of clause it will refer to only that which is no longer; or to that which has already passed away. And yet validity would come from such an absence.

12.3.6   The validity is always under question.

12.4.1   Validity occurs in termination of the contract.

12.4.2   The only manner to refer to the prerequisite for anything at all is in the act of termination, which allows for an awareness of what cannot be returned to; which in consequence may only be referred to as the void that would invalidate such reference.

12.4.3   Validity occurs as an ungraspable retraction.

12.4.4   The acceptance of a fund is validation — which is limited to that which it concerns, and no such other.

12.4.5   Funding is received in terms of reference to that which would invalidate that funded.

12.4.6   The funding has always already lapsed.

12.4.7   An entreatment for the funding corresponds to an awareness of the void that voids awareness. There is no end to termination.

12.5.1 The terms are of the void to which they signal.

12.5.2 If one is able to accept the possibility that such or such a contract may be qualified as void, and that regardless of terms it is impossible to be without a contract, then it has to be accepted that the void may not be set as such aside, but given into.

12.5.3 The void cannot be voided.

12.5.4 However of the void there may be something to mislead the apprehension into taking such for "such."

12.5.5 That which signifies the void is that which signifies as voided.

12.5.6 Every demonstration of the void is void by nature.

12.6.1   An awareness of the contract is awareness of the void that voids "the contract."

12.6.2   An adherence to "the contract" is exemplary default.

12.6.3   The contract will avoid its comprehension.

Of Finance

13.1.1   Although it be to come, the finance cannot be conceived as but behind one (past already).

13.1.2   That the finance be revealed as not the ground of that which is, but in the evident relief from that which was remains a sign of that to follow.

13.1.3   That from which and that to which the finance comes and goes cannot be present.

13.1.4   Relief is always past, and yet is always yet to come. For the present that remains remains unfounded.

13.1.5   The terms of finance have always already lapsed.

13.2.1   As the lapse that is already left behind is finance followed by a consciousness that follows its own lack of understanding by which terms may be contracted.

13.2.2   The finance comes to pass as separation from what cannot be remembered, to a consciousness to come.

13.2.3   That from which and that to which are one.

13.2.4   The finance would appear as disappearance that leaves only an example to refer to, which would have to be let go for the financial operation to continue.

13.2.5   The finance disappears in its provisioning of means of substitution. As correctly apprehended will these signs be turned away from and abandoned.

13.2.6   Finance cannot be conceived of as a product of its own facilitation; in that debt is not reducible to debt, reduced to debt, reduced to nothing.

13.2.7   It would follow that the only comprehension of the finance that may ever be achieved will be by means of that which signifies its absence.

13.2.8   The relevance of finance to the fact of that which is may be considered in the light of its delayed invalidation.

13.3.1 If a figure could be drawn for the perception of the finance it would have to be the figure of a spiral. But this figure must be seen as but a point along the edge of its own turning.

13.3.2 An alternative to such would be the figure of the debt as the circumference of a circle, with no centre to refer to; where the absence of proportion corresponds to an inherent need for finance.

13.4.1 There is no reason for the finance, such as "given in exchange for a particular good deed."

13.4.2 That the finance be is ground enough, and needs no other reason.

13.4.3 Any reason that is given to explain either the need or the potential for the finance will be reason to obstruct its operation.

13.4.4 The finance is refused in its own relevance to that which is provided. A refusal of this kind must coincide with its contingent operation.

13.4.5 A debt is both the product of and obstacle to finance.

13.5.1   The financial operations are expressions of the void that voids all matters of concern.

13.5.2   A financial operation of the kind that is of relevance to any situation will dissociate the same as such by funding for another.

13.5.3   The financial operations that release the self from worldly obligations are the countless generations of such figures of account that are recorded.

13.5.4   Difficult to comprehend is the necessity to leave that which the contract has provided. The appearance of a thing would be dependent on the fact that it be lost to the perceiver. Separation from that fact would be condition for it being to begin with.

13.5.5   The finance is conceived as the contraction of examples of endebtment, which may only be relieved by its continued operation. Thus its relevance to debt is both as that which gives, and that which takes away.

13.5.6   To entreat the operation of the finance must the consciousness in debt renounce all matters of concern — that is, including the concern that is for finance.

13.5.7   The finance is not given when or where one might decide it would be useful, but according to a need that is not given to make sense of.

13.6.1 The acceptance of the terms allows the universe to be. Its slow emergence corresponds to an imperative that separates the consciousness from everything that was to that which cannot be predicted.

13.6.2 The imperative would generate the funding.

13.6.3 The imperative necessitates the loss of what was given, in exchange for the appearance of whatever else might be. It may only be perceived in the reflection of its singular resultants, and not ever shown directly.

13.6.4 The imperative is heeded by refusing to maintain the least attachment whatever has been offered, and allowing it to offer such or such in separation from that offered. To obey is to renounce the world as given by the contract.

13.6.5 To follow the imperative is not to take control of that which happens, but to let the matter be.

13.6.6 The imperative may not be disobeyed in certain instances that signify itself. Though thus heeded when it must be, their significance is easy to pass over. Those however who have recognised their import will be held in preparation for whatever may be asked of them in future.

13.6.7 Follow the imperative regardless.

13.7.1   It is the finitude of finance that both validates and voids its operation.

13.7.2   The potential to refinance coincides with the financial operation, and as long as this continues. This potential is invalid if assumed as something given in advance of realisation.

13.7.3   A reality may not precede, but presupposes its acceptance.

13.7.4   The necessity for finance corresponds to the contingency of terms.

13.7.5   The finance brings about such innovation as the beating of a heart, which beating signifies what cannot be returned to.

13.7.6   Finance is the endless operation that brings end to that which cannot be remembered, leaving instances of debt that have no origin to which to be returned.

13.7.7   That the finance be refinance is a consequence of having no commencement to return to.

13.7.8   Nothing reappears beyond the finance.

Of the Lapse

14.1.1   If the operation that allows for debt be recognised as having passed already, then the consciousness to which it has resulted has no option but to follow its own absence of attention to the lapse that leaves it groundless.

14.1.2   The lapse is the beginning of the contract, in the sense that this be from the first unfounded.

14.1.3   The debt remains a signal of that lapse by which it came to be considered.

14.1.4   The lapse occurs as finance.

14.2.1 That which would enable the perception of the fact that it enables such already has already drawn away from its inadequate perception. This will nonetheless remain, as the provisional account of a financial operation.

14.2.2 The lapse is to be understood in terms of a deficiency of funding.

14.2.3 The groundlessness of debt appears in reference to the lapse that leaves no memory to return to.

14.2.4 It is not to the specific obligations that a consciousness in debt must be attentive — but the fundamental lapse which has already left them void.

14.2.5 There is no memory of the lapse.

14.3.1 Were it not for the originary lapse there would be nothing to consider.

14.3.2 The lapse could be defined as the immemorable first cause that may continue to effect the world as finance. Thus the relevance of finance to the presence of the world will only deepen the irreparably lost cause by which it came to be committed.

14.3.3 The figure to be drawn is of a mythical first time that leaves an incremental absence to return to.

14.3.4 The diverse specifications are so many indications of the fundamental lapse that has no meaning save as cause for the production of such means of indication.

14.3.5 The blueness of the sky is an uncanny indication of the lapse. It may as such be seen as irredeemable prehistory.

14.3.6 The lapse is what enables the appearance of the day, and of the nighttime.

14.3.7 The lapse by which the world has been provided will continue to evade the kind of fragile speculation it enables; in that such is not a thing, but an ongoing termination.

14.4.1   The lapse may not be recognised as such without increasing such as need for recognition.

14.4.2   The terms are consequential to the lapse for which they signify both end and alteration.

14.4.3   An apparent recognition of the lapse as the condition for whatever is must signify its deeper implication. The terms implied are pertinent to all that is perceivable at present; but to explicate these terms would be to implicate another kind of immanent condition to adhere to.

14.4.4   The terms implied are not to be referred to to decide upon the circumstance at hand, but irreparably implied in its appearance to begin with. The perception of whatever comes before has been enabled by what cannot be remembered.

14.4.5   Inherent to the fact that there be something to consider are however many terms that have contracted in a past of which no memory may ever have existed; and which cannot be conceived except in terms that are of relevance to "debt" and "absolution."

14.4.6   That which is supposed as the condition for the fact that there be any thing at all may be conceived in the contraction of such secondary terms as have disqualified whatever went before such observation.

14.4.7   That the universe is debt is said to signify the fact that it comes after.

14.5.1 The lapsing of the deadline is a fundamental breach that has to lead to termination of the contract. It is critical therefore to the effective operation of the contract; or is critical as such an operation. The contract will imply its own occasional disruption.

14.5.2 A breach of contract would allow for the emergence of a consequence that cannot be predicted.

14.5.3 Only following a breach may something be.

14.5.4 The deadline always alters as it nears.

14.5.5 The approaching of the deadline slowly separates the world from its ongoing dissolution. It determines all that is, as well as all that is no longer.

14.5.6 The postponement of the deadline brings the universe to light.

14.5.7 A sentence would decide another deadline.

14.5.8 Such a deadline is always already over.

14.6.1   An awareness of the contract is awareness of the lapse to which the contract has translated.

14.6.2   The lapse is irreversible, and happens as a fact to which one has to come to terms.

14.6.3   The lapse is both the need for and effect of termination.

14.6.4   The relevance of death to the reception of the world may not be presently made clear.

Termination

15.1.1   The account may not be settled by whatever other means than termination.

15.1.2   Attention to this world and this world only means to follow in default and draw continuous damnation.

15.1.3   The significance of terms is otherworldly.

15.2.1 An era will conclude in the arrival of a figure to refer to.

15.2.2 As provided by the contract will the cooling of the cosmos leave no room for the provisions of the contract. But perhaps within this absence will the future of the contract find its reason.

15.2.3 The final judgement is ongoing.

15.3.1 Every figure in the book will be a judgement that decides between one version and the next.

15.3.2 Death and judgement strictly coincide.

15.3.3 The judgments that arrive will be inscribed in terms for life in the account book.

15.3.4 Investments are a consequence of death.

15.4.1   The fulfilment of the promise is a promise to fulfil.

15.4.2   The beginning has no end.

15.4.3   The nature of the contract is to alter.

15.5.1　The image of the law implied its breaking. But unable to transcend his own humanity projected on the image of the golden calf had Moses failed to understand the fragments. Their significance would open to a later age that recognised itself in his hypocrisy and pride. Whereby the punishments were lifted.

15.6.1 A term is both an end and a beginning.

Index of Names

Abraham 3.4.3.
acceptance 1.5.1, 2.1.1, 2.3.4, 2.5.3, 2.5.4, 2.5.6, 2.5.7, 2.8.3, 2.9.5, 2.12.6, 3.7.1, 5.1.1, 5.4.3, 5.7.1, 5.10.1, 6.2.5, 8.7.1, 10.1.3, 10.2.3, 12.4.4, 13.6.1, 13.7.3.
account 2.9.6, 5.15.2, 6.1.4, 6.7.1, 6.7.2, 6.7.3, 7, 8.3.2, 14.2.1, 15.1.1, 15.3.3.
accountability 3.1.1, 3.1.2.
accounting 7.1.1, 7.1.2, 7.2.2, 7.2.6, 7.6.7, 7.8.1, 8.8.2.
Adam 1.3.5.
adherence 2.5.5, 2.6.10, 2.8.1, 3.2.3, 3.4.4, 6.4.1, 6.4.4, 6.4.5, 6.5.2, 7.2.2, 9.3.1, 12.6.2.
agreement 2.5.3, 2.5.6, 2.9.7, 2.10.2, 2.10.4, 5.5.5, 5.6.2, 5.8.3, 6.4.3, 8.7.6.
anything 2.4.2, 2.7.1, 2.11.4, 4.6.4, 5.7.1, 5.14.5, 8.4.1, 8.7.9, 12.4.2.
appearance 2.13.8, 3.2.3, 3.3.3, 5.3.1, 5.4.2, 7.6.4, 8.7.4, 10.5.3, 11.4.1, 13.5.4, 13.6.3, 14.3.6, 14.4.4.
apple 8.4.2.
approach 1.4.1, 11.3.6, 11.5.2.
approximation 3.1.4, 5.7.2, 7.5.3.
atmosphere 1.1.3.
atom 5.7.2.
attention 2.4.1, 7.6.1, 12.2.1, 14.1.1, 15.1.5.
awareness 1.2.2, 1.4.3, 2.1.1, 2.2.3, 2.2.4, 2.5.4, 2.12.1, 2.12.2, 3.7.4, 4.3.9, 6.9.5, 6.10.2, 10.2.5, 10.4.2, 10.5.7, 12.4.2, 12.4.7, 12.6.1, 14.6.1.
beginning 1.2.4, 2.1.1, 3.8.1, 3.8.2, 8.3.2, 10.5.4, 14.1.2, 15.4.2, 15.6.1.
bird 5.10.3.
blindness 4.2.7, 5.17.2.
book 5.15.2, 7.1.4, 7.2.3, 7.3.4, 15.3.1, 15.3.3.
breach 1.3.5, 5.16.3, 14.5.1, 14.5.2, 14.5.3.
calculation 5.7.1, 7.4.4, 7.5.3, 11.1.3.
cause 1.1.5, 1.2.4, 2.3.2, 2.13.8, 5.8.5, 7.5.5, 7.6.3, 7.6.5, 8.5.1, 11.3.4, 14.3.2, 14.3.4.
circle 13.3.2.
clause 2.3.6, 2.9.11, 3.3.2, 3.3.3, 7.8.3, 12.3.5.

closure 3.3.1.
cloud 5.10.3.
commitment 1.1.1, 4.1.4, 4.5.3, 7.3.1, 8.11.10.
conception 1.3.1, 1.3.4, 2.3.1, 2.3.3, 2.3.4, 2.3.5, 2.5.4, 2.6.2, 3.1.1, 3.1.4, 10.2.5, 10.4.1, 10.4.2.
concern 2.6.8, 4.2.6, 5.8.1, 5.11.6, 6.1.1, 6.1.3, 6.2.3, 7.3.6, 7.8.2, 7.8.3, 8.1.5, 10.2.3, 12.3.4, 13.5.1, 13.5.6.
condition 2.7.2, 2.11.1, 2.12.2, 2.14.3, 2.14.4, 3.1.2, 4.7.2, 5.2.1, 5.12.5, 6.5.5, 6.7.5, 8.4.5, 8.10.8, 9.1.3, 10.2.2, 10.3.1, 10.3.2, 10.3.6, 10.4.5, 14.4.3, 14.4.6.
conscience 2.6.5, 5.10.2, 5.10.3, 6.6.4, 8.10.2, 11.2.4.
consciousness 1.3.1, 2.12.2, 5.8.5, 7.3.6, 8.1.4, 8.2.3, 8.5.3, 8.13.6, 9.2.2, 13.2.1, 13.2.2, 13.5.6, 13.6.1, 14.1.1, 14.2.4.
consideration 2.11.2, 4, 5.1.1, 5.3.1, 5.6.3, 5.11.4, 6.7.4, 8.13.2, 10.5.2.
context 3.1.3, 3.1.4.
contingency 2.13.7, 13.7.4.
contraction 1.1.1, 2.2.6, 2.5.4, 2.8.5, 2.8.6, 2.13.1, 2.13.4, 3.1.4, 3.6.4, 5.6.3, 5.8.1, 5.12.3, 5.13.1, 5.15.2, 6.7.3, 7.1.3, 7.2.3, 7.3.5, 8.2.3, 8.4.1, 8.5.2, 8.7.3, 8.8.7, 8.9.2, 9.2.1, 9.2.2, 11.3.6, 12.3.2, 13.5.5, 14.4.6.
cosmos 3.4.1, 15.2.2.

credit 6.3.3, 6.3.4, 6.3.5, 6.3.7.
day 14.3.6.
deadline 10.5.4, 14.5.1, 14.5.4, 14.5.5, 14.5.6, 14.5.7, 14.5.8.
death 1.1.2, 1.3.1, 8.12.2, 8.12.5, 12.2.1, 14.6.4, 15.3.2, 15.3.4.
debt 5.6.1, 5.12.3, 6.9.3, 7.1.1, 7.2.1, 7.2.3, 7.3.5, 7.3.6, 7.3.7, 7.4.1, 7.4.4, 7.4.6, 7.6.4, 8, 9.2.2, 9.2.5, 10.1.1, 10.2.2, 10.4.4, 11.3.1, 13.2.6, 13.3.2, 13.4.5, 13.5.5, 13.5.6, 13.7.6, 14.1.1, 14.1.3, 14.2.3, 14.2.4, 14.5.5, 14.4.7.
decision 2.8.4, 12.2.1.
default 1.3.5, 2.12.2, 8.7.9, 9.1.4, 9.3.4, 10, 11.2.4, 11.5.1, 12.6.2, 15.1.2.
determination 1.3.1, 2.4.2, 2.5.5, 2.13.1, 2.13.6, 3.1.1, 5.2.2, 5.3.2, 5.8.1, 8.4.2.
difference 1.3.2, 3.2.2, 7.5.4, 7.5.5, 10.1.3, 10.4.5, 10.4.6, 11.
dysfunction 5.8.6, 10.3.3.
emergence 5.7.2, 5.14.3, 13.6.1, 14.5.2.
endebtment 4.1.5, 8.3.1, 8.3.2, 8.3.3, 8.4.2, 8.8.6, 9.2.1, 13.5.5.
entreatment 5.11.5, 5.11.6, 12.4.7.
entry 7.2.2, 7.2.6, 7.3.4, 7.3.5, 7.4.2.
equivalence 7.5.1.
era 11.3.1, 15.2.1.
error 7.6.7, 8.8.2, 10.5.1.

everything 2.2.1, 3.2.5, 5.3.3, 5.7.4, 5.11.7, 8.2.5, 8.11.1, 8.11.2, 9.3.3, 10.1.3, 11.4.1, 13.6.1.
example 2.2.6, 2.3.5, 2.3.6, 5.1.4, 5.2.4, 5.3.2, 5.6.1, 5.7.1, 5.14.3, 7.6.2, 8.3.2, 8.6.2, 13.2.4, 13.5.5.
exchange 7.5.1, 7.5.3, 13.4.1.
expression 1.4.2, 2.4.5, 2.12.6, 3.2.4, 5.1.2, 5.7.3, 5.14.4, 6.5.2, 6.5.3, 7.5.3, 8.10.4, 9.1.1, 11.5.3, 13.5.1.
facilitation 8.3.5, 13.2.6.
facility 5.1.1, 5.1.4, 5.2.1, 5.3.1, 5.4.1, 5.5.2, 5.5.5, 5.7.4, 5.8.1, 5.9.4, 5.9.5, 5.11.3, 5.11.4, 5.13.2, 5.14.2, 5.14.6, 5.14.4, 5.16.1, 6.2.4, 8.3.5, 10.3.3, 11.3.1, 11.3.2.
fact 2.6.4, 3.1.4, 7.1.4, 7.1.5, 7.6.4, 8.5.2, 13.2.8, 13.5.4, 14.2.1, 14.4.5, 14.4.6, 14.6.2.
faith 1.3.2, 3.4.4.
figure 4.5.5, 4.7.4, 5.14.2, 5.14.4, 5.15.2, 6.7.4, 7.2.2, 7.2.3, 7.3.2, 7.3.5, 7.5.4, 7.6.2, 7.6.6, 7.6.7, 7.7.1, 7.7.2, 7.7.3, 7.8.2, 7.8.3, 8.2.4, 8.5.4, 8.12.3, 11.2.7, 11.5.4, 12.1.1, 13.3.1, 13.3.2, 13.5.3, 14.3.3, 15.2.1, 15.3.1.
finance 1.2.6, 5.3.5, 7.1.3, 8.2.3, 8.3.3, 8.5.4, 8.9.4, 8.10.7, 9.3.4, 10.3.4, 10.4.7, 11.3.1, 12.2.1, 13, 14.1.4, 14.3.2.
flower 5.10.3.
forbidding 1.3.2, 2.8.3, 5.16.1, 5.16.2, 5.16.3, 5.16.4, 5.16.5, 5.17.1, 5.17.2, 5.17.3, 11.4.2, 11.4.3.
forgetting 10.4.1, 10.4.5.
formulation 2.6.4, 3.1.4, 5.13.6, 7.1.3, 7.2.3, 11.4.3.
foundation 5.12.3, 8.4.4, 9.1.3, 10.4.4.
freedom 2.14.4, 6.1.2, 6.7.5.
fulfilment 1.5.2, 2.3.4, 2.4.7, 2.7.1, 2.7.4, 2.13.1, 3.6.1, 4.2.1, 4.3.6, 5.1.3, 5.12.2, 7.2.3, 8.13.5, 10.5.2, 10.5.3, 11.3.5, 15.4.1.
function 3.1.3, 3.3.1, 3.3.2, 3.3.6.
fund 4.3.3, 5.5.6, 5.5.8, 5.7.2, 5.8.1, 5.13.6, 5.15.3, 6.1.2, 6.2.4, 7.5.5, 8.7.3, 10.2.6, 12.4.4.
funding 2.2.2, 2.3.5, 2.6.7, 2.10.4, 2.11.3, 4.1.4, 4.3.4, 5, 6.1.3, 6.2.2, 6.2.4, 6.4.1, 6.6.2, 6.7.1, 6.7.2, 6.9.1, 6.9.3, 7.5.6, 8.2.6, 8.5.2, 9.1.3, 9.2.6, 10.3.3, 11.3.4, 12.4.5, 12.4.6, 12.4.7, 13.5.2, 13.6.2, 14.2.2.
future 2.3.5, 2.13.8, 4.2.5, 4.2.7, 5.15.1, 5.15.3, 6.2.4, 6.3.1, 6.4.3, 6.5.1, 6.5.2, 6.7.1, 7.2.2, 7.2.6, 7.4.2, 8.10.2, 13.6.6, 15.2.2.
galaxies 5.4.1.
gas 1.1.3.
god 2.2.6, 8.6.3.
good 4.4.4, 5.6.3, 5.6.4.
guarantee 2.13.2, 5.12.4, 5.16.4, 6.8.1, 6.8.3, 10.6.3.
heart 13.7.5.
human 2.2.5, 2.2.6, 10.1.2.
hypocrisy 15.5.1.

identity 8.11.4, 8.11.7, 9.3.1, 9.3.2, 11.4.2.
illusion 2.5.3, 11.4.1.
image 1.3.3, 2.7.1, 3.2.3, 5.2.3, 5.7.2, 10.5.5, 11.3.6, 11.4.2, 11.4.3, 12.3.4, 15.5.1.
imperative 2.4.2, 2.6.9, 2.7.1, 4.5.3, 5.14.5, 13.6.1, 13.6.2, 13.6.3, 13.6.4, 13.6.5, 13.6.6, 13.6.7.
implication 2.9.8, 2.13.2, 2.14.3, 5.10.3, 5.15.1, 14.4.3.
incompletion 2.6.6, 3.6.2, 3.6.3.
incorporation 2.12.3.
indication 8.10.5, 12.3.1, 14.3.4, 14.3.5.
injunction 6.5.4.
interest 3.2.2, 5.8.6, 5.9.3, 8.11.3, 10.3.6.
interminate 2.11.4, 3.3.5, 7.5.7, 11.2.1, 11.2.2, 11.4.1, 11.4.2, 11.5.2, 11.5.3.
interpretation 3, 4.2.5, 4.5.6, 6.10.2, 7.1.4, 7.2.2, 7.2.3, 7.8.4, 12.1.2.
investment 2.10.3, 5.5.7, 5.8.2, 5.9.1, 6, 8.12.2, 10.3.5, 15.3.4.
investor 6.1.1, 6.1.2, 6.1.3, 6.5.5, 6.6.1.
judgement 10.1.2, 10.4.8, 15.2.3, 15.3.1, 15.3.2.
knowledge 1.3.2, 2.1.3, 2.3.4, 2.11.3.
lapse 2.10.4, 5.12.2, 13.2.1, 14.
law 1.3.2, 7.1.3, 15.5.1.

liability 2.1.2, 4.1.3, 4.1.6, 4.3.5, 4.3.6, 4.3.7, 4.3.9, 4.4.1, 7.5.4.
life 1.3.3, 2.6.2, 3.3.4, 11.2.4, 15.3.3.
light 1.1.3.
limit 4.1.2, 5.5.2, 5.5.6, 5.5.7, 8.12.2.
literature 7.1.3.
meaning 1.1.3, 2.2.6, 2.9.9, 3.1.4, 3.4.2, 8.8.4, 11.2.2, 11.4.1.
means 1.3.1, 2.9.3, 2.10.1, 3.2.4, 4.1.5, 4.5.4, 4.6.3, 5.5.5, 5.11.3, 6.2.5, 6.5.2, 7.4.5, 8.12.2, 11.1.3, 12.3.3, 13.2.5, 13.2.7, 14.3.4, 15.1.1.
method 7.1.1, 7.2.1, 7.2.2, 7.2.6, 7.3.1.
money 7.5.7.
Moses 15.5.1.
name 1.3.3, 6.7.3.
naming 1.3.1.
narration 7.1.3, 7.6.4.
necessity 2.13.5, 3.6.1, 5.2.1, 5.12.3, 8.2.1, 8.2.3, 8.5.4, 13.5.4, 13.7.4.
negotiation 7.2.1.
night 14.3.6.
nothing 1.1.1, 4.6.4, 5.1.1, 5.2.1, 5.3.5, 5.5.1, 5.5.2, 5.6.1, 5.6.4, 5.7.2, 5.10.1, 5.11.7, 5.12.4, 7.3.6, 8.1.2, 8.1.3, 8.1.5, 8.2.2, 8.2.3, 8.2.5, 8.2.7, 8.3.2, 11.2.7, 11.3.2, 13.7.8.
oath 2.8.1, 6.4.2, 6.4.3, 6.4.4, 6.5.1, 6.5.2.
obligation 1.2.7, 2.1.3, 2.3.6, 2.6.7, 2.8.2, 2.10.2, 4.1.5, 4.3.6,

4.4.1, 4.4.2, 4.4.3, 4.4.4, 4.4.5, 4.4.6, 4.5.1, 4.5.2, 4.5.4, 4.5.5, 4.5.2, 5.8.5, 5.9.2, 7.7.3, 8.5.2, 8.5.4, 8.8.7, 8.10.7, 8.11.4, 8.12.1, 8.12.2, 10.5.4, 11.5.2, 13.5.3, 14.2.4.
observation 5.13.4, 12.3.2, 14.4.6.
operation 2.2.2, 2.3.5, 2.14.2, 2.14.3, 4.2.2, 4.5.5, 4.6.5, 5.1.3, 5.1.5, 5.2.2, 5.2.3, 5.2.4, 5.3.2, 5.4.2, 5.13.1, 5.13.2, 5.15.1, 6.9.2, 8.2.3, 8.3.1, 8.4.2, 8.11.8, 8.12.1, 9.3.2, 10.3.3, 10.3.5, 10.4.7, 11.3.1, 11.3.3, 12.3.3, 13.2.4, 13.4.3, 13.4.4, 13.5.1, 13.5.2, 13.5.3, 13.5.5, 13.5.6, 13.7.1, 13.7.2, 13.7.6, 14.1.1, 14.2.1, 14.5.1.
origin 1, 5.14.5, 8.6.1, 8.6.2, 8.6.5, 8.10.2, 8.10.3, 9.1.2, 13.7.6.
past 1.2.5, 2.13.8, 3.7.1, 3.7.4, 5.13.1, 5.14.2, 5.14.4, 6.7.4, 8.9.2, 14.4.5.
payment 6.5.3, 7.3.6, 7.7.2, 7.7.4, 8.2.4, 8.5.5, 8.7.1, 8.7.5, 8.7.8, 8.7.9, 8.7.10, 8.9.6, 8.13.4, 8.13.5, 10.1.3, 10.1.5, 10.1.6, 10.4.6, 11.1.3, 11.2.4, 11.2.8, 11.5.4, 12.1.1, 12.1.2.
perception 2.2.3, 2.9.4, 3.3.2, 3.6.1, 4.2.7, 5.3.2, 8.3.4, 8.4.1, 9.4.1, 10.5.1, 12.3.3, 13.3.1, 14.2.1, 14.4.4.
performance 2.8.6, 2.14.1, 3.7.2, 5.1.2, 5.1.3, 5.11.4.
possession 1.3.1, 3.2.3, 5.9.4, 9.1.4, 9.2.6, 9.3.2, 10.3.5, 10.5.1.
potential 2.14.1, 3.6.4, 6.3.2, 6.6.1, 13.4.3, 13.7.2.
prehistory 8.12.2, 14.3.5.
preparation 1.3.2, 5.17.3, 10.2.3, 13.6.6.
presence 2.13.2, 2.13.3, 4.6.2, 5.3.2, 5.10.3, 7.3.6, 8.3.1, 8.4.5, 8.5.3, 8.5.4, 10.5.2, 10.5.6, 14.3.2.
present 3.7.1, 3.7.4, 6.5.1, 6.7.5, 12.3.1, 13.1.4, 14.4.3.
pressure 4.5.3, 7.3.7, 8.2.5, 8.7.7, 9.2.3, 10.7.1.
pride 10.5.5, 15.5.1.
production 5.1.5, 5.12.2, 8.8.8, 8.10.1, 11.3.4, 14.3.4.
prohibition 1.3.1, 1.3.2, 1.3.3, 6.7.5.
promise 2.13.1, 3.4.3, 4.6.2, 4.7.4, 5.12.2, 5.16.5, 6.4.5, 6.5.1, 6.5.3, 6.8.1, 6.8.4, 7.3.4, 8.7.5, 8.13.2, 8.13.3, 8.13.4, 8.13.6, 10.5.2, 11.3.4, 15.4.1.
property 9.
provision 2.7.2, 2.9.3, 4.2.3, 4.2.4, 4.2.5, 4.2.6, 4.2.7, 4.3.1, 6.5.1, 15.2.2.
punishment 10.1.2, 15.5.1.
rainbow 1.4.2.
realisation 2.9.3, 5.1.4, 13.7.2.
reality 5.12.3, 6.3.4, 9.3.4, 13.7.3.

reason 1.1.4, 1.1.5, 2.11.1, 5.8.4, 7.6.3, 8.2.3, 13.4.1, 13.4.2, 13.4.3, 15.2.2.
reception 4.2.4, 6.2.5, 14.6.4.
recognition 7.4.1, 8.1.6, 9.1.1, 10.4.4, 10.4.6, 11.1.5, 14.4.1, 14.4.3.
reduction 8.8.8, 10.1.3.
reference 5.13.1, 5.13.5, 7.4.4, 8.10.4, 12.4.2, 12.4.5.
reflection 4.6.4, 5.14.2, 5.15.1, 13.6.3.
renewal 3.8.1, 6.3.6.
resignation 2.5.6, 5.4.3, 5.11.1, 5.12.2, 8.5.5, 10.1.2.
resources 4.1.3, 4.1.5, 4.3.1, 5.8.1, 10.3.2.
return 2.1.1, 3.8.2, 6.1.1, 6.1.4, 6.6.4, 6.7.3, 6.8.1, 8.12.5.
science 7.1.3.
self 2.12.3, 2.12.5, 7.7.3, 8.11.4, 8.11.8, 8.12.1, 10.1.3, 13.5.3.
sentence 3.5.6, 10.4.9, 12.3.5, 14.5.7.
separation 5.4.2, 8.11.9, 8.12.4, 11.1.4, 13.2.2, 13.5.4, 13.6.4.
sign 1.3.2, 2.4.7, 4.2.4, 6.5.3, 6.5.4, 7.4.1, 7.4.2, 8.13.5, 13.1.2, 13.2.5.
signature 1.6.1.
significance 1.4.3, 2.3.8, 2.9.9, 2.9.11, 3.1.4, 3.2.4, 3.3.1, 3.4.3, 4.2.7, 5.17.1, 6.8.5, 7.5.2, 13.6.6, 15.1.3, 15.5.1.
signing 2.5.6, 2.5.7, 2.10.5, 2.12.4, 2.13.3, 4.3.8, 5.1.1, 6.5.3, 7.4.5.
sky 14.3.5.
something 2.9.6, 3.5.3, 4.6.1, 4.7.1, 5.7.2, 5.12.4, 5.12.5, 5.16.4, 6.3.6, 6.8.2, 6.8.5, 7.6.1, 8.4.3, 8.4.4, 8.7.9, 9.1.2, 10.5.4, 12.5.4, 13.7.2, 14.4.5, 14.5.3.
space 1.3.3, 2.11.2, 4.3.7, 4.3.8, 7.5.1, 7.6.2.
speculation 2.2.7, 6.2.4, 14.3.7.
spiral 13.3.1.
star 1.1.2, 3.4.3, 3.4.5, 5.7.3.
stone 5.7.3.
subject 1.3.1, 3.2.1, 5.8.1, 8.1.5, 8.6.3, 8.7.9, 8.11.2, 8.11.3, 8.11.4, 8.11.5, 8.11.8, 8.12.3, 9.3.4, 10.5.4.
substance 5.6.1, 8.8.1.
sum 5.5.3, 5.5.4.
survival 2.6.10, 3.3.6.
swearing 2.8.1, 6.3.7.
term 1.1.3, 1.2.3, 1.4.1, 1.4.2, 1.5.1, 2.1.1, 2.1.2, 2.3.1, 2.3.2, 2.3.6, 2.3.7, 2.3.9, 2.4.3, 2.4.4, 2.4.5, 2.4.6, 2.4.7, 2.5.2, 2.5.3, 2.5.6, 2.6.2, 2.6.3, 2.6.11, 2.6.12, 2.7.4, 2.8.3, 2.8.6, 2.9.2, 2.9.5, 2.9.8, 2.9.9, 2.9.10, 2.11.3, 2.11.4, 2.12.2, 2.12.3, 2.12.5, 2.12.6, 2.13.1, 2.13.5, 2.13.6, 2.13.8, 2.14.2, 3.1.3, 3.1.4, 3.2.1, 3.2.3, 3.2.5, 3.3.1, 3.3.2, 3.3.6, 3.5.2, 3.6.1, 3.6.4, 3.7.2, 3.8.1, 4.1.2, 4.1.4, 4.2.1, 4.3.1, 4.3.7, 5.1.1, 5.1.2, 5.1.3, 5.4.3, 5.5.1, 5.5.7, 5.6.3, 5.6.4, 5.7.1, 5.8.1, 5.8.3, 5.9.5,

5.10.2, 5.11.1, 5.11.2, 5.12.2, 5.13.1, 5.13.2, 5.13.4, 5.14.4, 5.17.1, 6.2.1, 6.2.3, 6.2.5, 6.3.1, 6.4.1, 6.6.1, 6.7.3, 6.7.4, 6.9.1, 6.10.2, 7.1.1, 7.2.1, 7.2.3, 7.2.4, 7.2.5, 7.3.1, 7.5.1, 7.5.4, 7.8.1, 8.1.5, 8.4.3, 8.5.2, 8.5.3, 8.5.4, 8.7.2, 8.8.3, 8.10.1, 8.10.6, 8.10.7, 8.10.8, 8.11.5, 8.11.10, 8.12.4, 8.13.1, 8.13.5, 9.1.1, 9.2.1, 10.1.2, 10.1.3, 10.2.3, 10.2.6, 10.4.2, 10.4.6, 10.4.7, 10.5.3, 10.6.2, 10.7.1, 11.1.1, 11.1.4, 11.2.1, 11.2.3, 11.3.1, 11.3.3, 11.3.5, 11.4.4, 11.5.1, 12.1.2, 12.2.1, 12.4.5, 12.5.1, 12.5.2, 13.1.5, 13.2.1, 13.6.1, 13.7.4, 14.2.2, 14.4.2, 14.4.3, 14.4.4, 14.4.5, 14.4.6, 14.6.2, 15.1.3, 15.3.3, 15.6.1.
termination 1.2.4, 2.5.2, 2.6.12, 3.8.2, 4.5.2, 5.13.1, 8.7.7, 8.11.4, 8.12.3, 10.1.3, 12.2.2, 12.3.4, 12.4.1, 12.4.2, 12.4.7, 14.3.7, 14.5.1, 14.6.3, 15.
terminology 3.1.4.
text 3.2.2, 3.4.1, 3.4.2, 3.5.5, 3.6.4, 3.7.1.
thing 1.3.3, 2.3.5, 2.9.4, 2.9.5, 2.13.2, 2.13.3, 4.7.1, 5.1.1, 5.2.1, 5.2.3, 5.3.3, 5.3.5, 5.4.1, 5.4.3, 5.5.3, 5.7.2, 5.13.2, 5.13.5, 6.2.6, 6.6.1, 6.9.1, 6.9.2, 7.5.1, 7.5.6, 8.1.1, 8.2.1, 8.4.3, 8.7.2, 8.9.3, 9.4.2, 10.5.3, 11.4.1, 13.5.4, 14.3.7, 14.4.6.
threat 4.3.2.

total 7.7.2.
totality 2.10.1, 5.3.2, 11.4.1.
transgression 1.3.1.
understanding 1.2.5, 1.4.1, 2.1.2, 2.11.3, 2.13.1, 2.13.4, 3.5.1, 3.5.2, 5.5.1, 5.5.7, 5.11.6, 5.12.1, 5.14.5, 6.5.5, 6.7.3, 6.10.1, 7.2.3, 7.3.5, 8.4.2, 8.6.2, 8.9.3, 8.12.2, 10.2.3, 10.2.4, 10.2.5, 11.2.4, 11.2.6, 11.3.1, 12.2.1, 12.3.3, 13.2.1.
universe 1.1.1, 1.2.3, 1.2.6, 2.2.3, 2.10.5, 5.7.3, 5.12.2, 5.14.3, 8.8.6, 9.1.2, 9.1.4, 13.6.1, 14.4.7, 14.5.6.
validation 10.2.3, 10.2.4, 12.4.4.
validity 5.14.2, 5.16.4, 12.2.1, 12.3.3, 12.3.4, 12.3.5, 12.3.6, 12.4.1, 12.4.3.
vision 1.1.3, 1.1.4, 2.4.2, 2.9.7, 3.4.1, 4.2.7, 4.5.1.
void 8.2.3, 8.2.4, 8.10.4, 8.10.5, 10.2.2, 10.5.4, 11.5.3, 12, 13.5.1.
wealth 4.2.1, 4.2.4, 6.10.3.
will 5.8.1, 5.8.3, 5.9.2, 11.4.1.
womb 2.6.1.
word 3.1.4.
world 1.3.1, 1.4.1, 2.1.3, 2.1.5, 2.5.8, 2.7.1, 3.1.1, 3.2.1, 3.2.3, 3.2.4, 3.3.1, 3.3.2, 3.3.3, 4.3.5, 4.4.3, 5.2.3, 5.6.3, 5.6.5, 5.15.1, 6.1.2, 6.1.3, 6.8.4, 7.2.2, 7.4.6, 8.3.1, 8.3.2, 8.7.4, 8.11.3, 8.12.1, 10.4.2, 10.4.3, 10.4.5, 10.5.3, 10.5.4, 10.5.5, 11.1.4, 12.2.1,

12.3.4, 13.6.4, 14.3.2, 14.3.7,
14.5.5, 14.6.4, 15.1.2.
worth 2.9.3, 6.7.4, 6.8.1, 6.8.2,
6.8.3, 6.8.4, 6.8.5, 6.9.1, 6.9.2,
6.9.4, 6.9.5, 7.4.1, 7.5.2.

"W. dreams, like Phaedrus, of an army of thinker-friends, thinker-lovers. He dreams of a thought-army, a thought-pack, which would storm the philosophical Houses of Parliament. He dreams of Tartars from the philosophical steppes, of thought-barbarians, thought-outsiders. What distance would shine in their eyes!"

— Lars Iyer

www.ingramcontent.com/pod-product-compliance
Lightning Source LLC
Chambersburg PA
CBHW071700170426
43195CB00039B/2400